MW00657422

"In *Marriage is a Business*, Dr. Secres_ ... . -. p-..--.
ful tools and strategies for forming and sustaining a successful marriage. Her approach is not only logical and clear, it is enjoyable and immediately applicable. The insights and activities Dr. Secrest offers are sure to enhance the life of any couple."

—Rick Carson, Clinical Member and Approved Supervisor, American Association for Marriage and Family Therapy, Author of *Taming Your Gremlin*® and *A Master Class in Gremlin-Taming*®

"This book details an innovative and creative way of conceptualizing marital therapy. Likening couples counseling to a business model is both pragmatic and nonthreatening, especially for those individuals new to therapy who may be apprehensive about having to talk too much initially about their feelings. The added dimension of cognitive-behavioral interventions to promote change is an empirically validated approach which also may be less stressful for couples who are perhaps a bit nervous regarding traditional talk therapy. I can't wait to try this out with my patients!"

—Anne N. Weinberg, PhD, Psychologist, Private Practice

"Viewing marriage as a business is a brilliant model to help couples focus on the issues that need to be addressed rather than getting side-tracked into personal attacks. This book is well written with useful, practical tips and ideas that can be easily understood and applied to every relationship."

—Shaalon Joules, PhD, Psychologist, Private Practice

"*Marriage is a Business* answers the frequently asked question, "But how do I do that?", when couples are told to manage their emotions more effectively. This handbook is practical and easy to read, with excellent real world examples of relationship issues that many couples face and the techniques used to negotiate those turbulent emotional waters. I highly recommend this guide to both therapists and couples who are trying to make things better. Well done!"

—Marcus M. Greenwood, LPC, Private Practice

"*Marriage is a Business* is a fresh look at the art of partnership, conscious goal setting, and problem solving within a committed relationship. Dr. Secrest's practical steps and comprehensive "How To" guidelines are valuable in any stage of marriage. I will highly recommend this to many of my coaching clients."

—JEANIE BROSIUS KING, GLOBAL LIFE COACH…FOR A LIFE YOU LOVE!

"Dr. Secrest, talented as a writer and psychologist, explains in her book, *Marriage is a Business*, a clear and understandable reason why many marriages fail. She states that marriages are not meant to serve our personal needs but must be run like a business where both partners 'pull their own weight' and work to meet the needs of the relationship. *Marriage is a Business* is an important resource for teaching marriage fundamentals and should be a must-read for all couples."

—PEGGY MCMAHON, PHD, PSYCHOLOGIST, PRIVATE PRACTICE

"A practical, no nonsense approach to the 'business' of marriage. Provides concrete tools and easily understood concepts to help couples meet their mutual goals."

—KENNETH WISE, PSYD, PRIVATE PRACTICE

"Well written and easy to read. The worksheets are beneficial in keeping you on track. The book is practical and appealing in its simplicity. I think it's a must read for any couple."

—REBECCA B.

Marriage
is a Business

A Logical Approach to the
Psychology of Relationships

Jenny Secrest, PhD
with Karin Bruckner, MA

www.jennysecrestphd.com
www.marriageisabusiness.com

ISBN: 978-0-9857265-0-8
Library of Congress Control Number: 2012914727
Designed by Mayfly Design and typeset in MillerText

Printed in the United States of America
First Printing: 2013

17 16 15 14 13   5 4 3 2 1

This book was written for those who have found—or hope to find—the gift of a deep loving relationship and would like to benefit from a strong dose of logic.

Dedicated to Dylan ... maximize life!

Contents

Preface

Psychology, in all its glorious complexity, is the study of the individual. This complexity is found in all the features that make each person unique—our complex brain and elaborate emotional system, for instance—and then is amplified by environmental influences. To attempt to discuss the full range of human intricacy is far beyond the scope of this book. In fact, discussion of the abstract and infinite ways psychology impacts our lives could fill countless libraries.

Rather than exercising such a broad reach, the goal of this book is to reduce such complexity. This is accomplished by first looking to the world of business—a world filled with concrete goals, defined processes, and recognizable structures designed to work together to produce a successful outcome. Commonly used business practices familiar to many in today's workforce are presented as effective tools for managing the daily requirements and conflicts of married life.

A Business Model? Really??

By far the most common reaction to *Marriage is a Business* is one of slight skepticism. Why would anyone try to apply business techniques to marriage, or any kind of relationship for that matter? Isn't it comparing apples to oranges, board rooms to bedrooms, profits to passion? The fact that few can see the similarities between running a successful business and navigating a successful marriage attests to the current lack of realism in our culture's view of how to achieve a happy marriage.

My approach to establishing an effective foundation for a marriage that works comes from over 20 years of work as a therapist. In that time, I have defined and refined the tools that I believe make the most difference to couples whose relationships are in trouble. These tools are not emotion-based therapeutic improvisations or pathways for exploring past traumas and hurts. While they and other valid therapeutic approaches all have their place, my vision for helping couples achieve a strong relationship centers on handling the business of marriage very, very well, and this requires a lot of self-discipline, a strong work ethic, and yes, some business savvy. I believe this book fills a gap that has been left by other self-help and therapeutic approaches. It highlights the importance of being able to **manage** one's self and one's relationships, and addresses problems and obstacles others do not.

Over time, there have been innumerable requests from my clients for "something in writing." Some felt a need to have a reference in hand as they negotiated the challenges of daily married life at home, while others wanted to pass on information to a friend whose marriage was struggling. Thus, this book was born to fill a concrete need expressed by the real people with whom I've had the privilege of working, in the belief that it represents a similar need within the larger population with its persistent 50% divorce rate.

A Psychological Primer

Along with practical skills, a good marriage also requires a certain level of self awareness and the ability to balance and integrate our thoughtful selves with our emotional selves. Thus, a second crucial element of this book is a simple, easy, straightforward understanding of how individuals can manage themselves psychologically, both as independent selves and within a relationship.

The basic psychological concepts presented here are limited to thoughts and feelings, and the interplay between the two. Only when a person comes to understand this interplay within them-selves (i.e., learn psychological self-management) can he or she then explore more complicated psychological issues. My business model requires people to keep their intellect continuously switched on as they manage their emotions through adulthood and learn how to integrate thoughts and feelings. When people decide to include marriage in their lives—an important yet complex life option—this integration of heart and mind must be extended from internal self-management to external relationship management.

When exploring any new field of knowledge, one must learn the basics before advancing to more in-depth material. Thus, this book is meant to serve as a psychological primer with information that is fundamental to more advanced psychological knowledge. To explore any additional psychological complexities would tax the novice reader of marital self-help material, add unnecessary con-fusion, and perhaps even sabotage any new understandings the reader might glean from the information presented. As a result, readers will not find discussions of the roles of love, sex, intimacy, or other typical relationship topics in this book. Of course these psy-chological themes are important to building a deep, high-quality relationship. However, this book was written specifically to help readers master a simple, basic, initial step toward self- and rela-tionship management.

Too many divorces continue to take place; too much emotional devastation continues to negatively affect too many men, women, and, of course, children. I have heard time and time again my cli-ents declare, "I think people need to know all this **before** they get married," or "I wish I had known all this awhile ago," and "I don't know what happened or what to do." This book was written to dis-pel the unwanted lack of information expressed in those statements and teach people how they can successfully enter into and maintain a marriage. Nothing more complex than that.

Our culture remains persistently unaware (or perhaps avoid-ant) of how few marriages last and make it to the traditional "til death do us part" wedding commitment. To achieve a lifetime of rewarding marriage, both partners need the tools, the commitment, and the discipline to integrate management of their thoughts, their feelings, and their relationship. I believe that with these elements in place, a marriage can flourish and bring much joy into the shared lives of committed couples.

Acknowledgments

First and foremost, hands down, and above all else, I wish to thank Karin Bruckner for all her help. She is the bona fide, experienced writer/author here. Karin helped me express my no nonsense, black-and-white, blunt passion for contributing to the world such that readers could hopefully find the information easy to understand and follow. I would not have tackled this project without her.

There are others I wish to thank as well. Thanks to Becca Marin, Nancy Branaman, and Diana Boone for their support, encouragement, and friendship. Thanks also to all who volunteered to read the manuscript and offer constructive ideas for improvements. Becca especially went way above expectations in offering a comprehensive and critical eye to polish the editing of this book. Ditto to Greg S. who, in addition to editing changes, also offered valuable information as to how this book could enable his relationship.

Finally, there are others who offered advice, direction, or guidance at just the right moments during the final phases of moving this book toward publication. Heartfelt thanks to Naomi and Larry Kryske, Benjamin Bruckner, Dylan Secrest, Tim Branaman, and Peggy McMahon.

Introduction

Many couples choose therapy at some stage during their relationship. Some come in because they want to strengthen a relationship that is already moving forward: "We get along, we just have some differences." Other couples come in to find solutions for much more difficult problems:

- They love each other, but they fight; in fact, they fight a lot!
- There is an absence of any affection and intimacy.
- Blended family issues threaten the marriage and child-rearing issues become a constant source of friction.
- There is a noticeable lack of time spent together: "He/she spends more time at work or with friends than with me."

Still other couples make their way to the therapist's office when it is almost too late—there has been an extramarital affair, or serious discussions about divorce have taken place.

Regardless of what state their marriage is in, couples do come in. But even when a marriage is on its last legs, the fact that both partners make an effort to choose a therapist, locate the office, and somehow find the courage to walk in and sit down shows that each person has some level of motivation and an interest in change. As they sit facing their therapist for the first time, the couple's hope is that no matter what challenges they walked in with, they will walk out with skills, solutions, and tools to help them feel better, to feel happy again. Many want to stay together and "make this thing work." Some are not sure what they want, but are willing to clarify goals and then try to achieve them.

This potential for change, no matter how small or tenuous, is an important element in bringing a marriage back to life. Once it is identified and acknowledged, a couple must then dedicate themselves to acquiring tools for managing themselves and their relationship. In therapy, there are a variety of ways to help couples do this. A walk down any bookstore's relationship self-help aisle offers a lot of information about how marital problems are approached. Primarily, a therapist will focus either on the intellectual identification of problems, the underlying emotional disconnect between the couple, or both. Some couples need more help at the cognitive, problem-solving level, while others need to focus on emotional connection through effective communication skills and emotional self-management. Most couples need help with both of these tasks.

This book is similar to others in that it, too, addresses both the intellectual and emotional levels of a relationship. It is different, though, in that it uses a model somewhat outside the realm of psychology to define a structure and foundation for marriage that is more often seen in the business world. In fact, this approach asks you to view your marriage as a working business. Early on in this book, the emphasis will be on the ways you can use your intellect and your rational thinking to create a foundation for your relationship based on a business plan to which you both agree. After this plan is established, we will explore how your emotions interface with this logical perspective and discuss the ways in which feelings can either enhance or sabotage the success of your relationship.

When marriage is envisioned as a corporate entity, focus is placed on factors that have been proven to optimize growth and success. Let's take a look at each of these factors to see how they are used in the business world. The factors are summarized in the following commitment statement which will serve to guide our discussion here in the Introduction and also later in the book as we address how each can contribute to the health of your marriage.

"We agree to become partners in joint ownership of a business with a vision and a plan, adopting policies and procedures which are developed during regularly scheduled board meetings and are achieved through skills of negotiating, compromising, and communicating."

Your Basic Company

We agree to become partners in joint ownership of a business with a vision and a plan...

In the beginning, the people who start a company have to find each other and identify their shared interests. They then agree to pool and invest their resources, time, and energy to become **business partners**. Ever hear someone described as "married to their job"? Such people often have a **vision** of what they would like to develop and one of their first jobs is to construct a **working plan** for turning their ideas into action, starting their business, and making it grow.

Suppose we take a moment now to think of what people actually do when they are starting a business. Some of the things they must consider and decide on are:

- Who are the investors, partners, and owners?
- What are the contributions each participant brings to the table?
- What resources are available right now?
- How will decisions be made? How much weight will each participant's vote carry?
- What are the working vision and the plan?

> ...adopting policies and procedures which are developed during regularly scheduled board meetings...

As the business partners get moving on bringing their vision to life, the prep work is carried out in a professional manner—that is to say, logically, objectively, and maturely. One main tool for much of this initial high-level decision making is the **board meeting**. Board meetings are where company owners discuss concerns and solve problems. At any big corporation, the executives make a date, sit down together, and follow a prepared agenda to deal with the issues at hand. The foundation for these discussions is the business plan that helps people visualize the path their company will take over the next year, the next five years, and so on. Projects designed to promote the company's vision are assigned to various members who then report back on their progress at future board meetings.

One of the first of these assigned projects typically involves the development of company **policies and procedures**. These basically represent a how-to manual for the company and can cover topics such as attendance, benefits, a code of conduct, discipline, and job descriptions.

> ...and are achieved through skills of negotiating, compromising...

Company owners and executives negotiate...sometimes, a lot! When they can't concur on a specific item, they **negotiate and compromise** until an agreed-upon solution is hammered out. Then they shake hands and move on to the next item of business. If for some reason there is no agreement on a certain item, no action can be taken because no one person has the exclusive authority to out-vote or overrule another. That item will be tabled for future discussion and progress in that area must wait until an agreement is forged.

…and communicating.

So that board members can feel confident that they understand each other fully—and to keep the board meetings from going on indefinitely—effective **communication skills** are practiced regularly. Executives are expected to be accomplished communicators with skills that include:

- The ability to express themselves clearly and accurately.
- Active listening, remembering to acknowledge the speaker and really hear what is being said.
- Thinking logically and minimizing any emotional response.
- Contributing constructive ideas to help move the discussion forward.
- Staying focused on the topic at hand.

To Summarize…

The point of this book is to offer a unique approach, one that likens marriage to a company or business. We're all familiar in some way or other with the typical business model. It's logical, not emotional, and focuses on growing the productivity of the partnership so that obstacles are overcome and benefits accrue to the business itself as well as the individuals involved.

Emotions are important; they are ultimately the reason that couples seek therapy in the first place. This book, however, begins with a more cognitive focus, using business as a model for relationship success. Once this foundation is laid in Part I, a discussion of how emotional connection fits into the "family business" is offered in Part II. Part III helps to combine both of these areas of learning and provides some real-life application, and Part IV ties it all together with some concluding thoughts that will help you stay motivated for bringing about productive change in your relationship. Be sure to check out the back of the book for some handy tips and quick-reference Partnership Tools you can print out and bring with you to your family business meetings.

Congratulations on making the choice to take action. Now get ready to learn a new and different paradigm for achieving success in marriage! It's time to get down to business.

Part I

And now, the marriage...or rather, the Business of Marriage!

So you decided to become entrepreneurs...or should I say, married! Developing and running a business is not child's play, and the same holds true for marriage. It requires commitment, dedication, trust, faith, and perseverance to create and maintain a solid foundation that will withstand the setbacks and losses we all must weather in life. The earlier you both begin doing the homework needed to build this foundation, the smoother and simpler your road together can be.

Key Elements

- Two business owners
- A single shared vision
- A working business plan
- Regular board meetings
- Policies and procedures
- Negotiation and compromise
- Effective communication

What happens when we take the basic aspects of developing, building, and operating a new business as described in the previous section and apply them to your marriage? This section will spell out specific steps that can bring your relationship in line with your needs and expectations as a couple.

Partners in Joint Ownership

Ownership, as applied to both business and your marriage, is all about managing the family business through forming a partnership that works together smoothly to develop and solidify the business. When two people build their relationship and then marry, each essentially contributes 50 percent of the resources. That is to say, each brings his or her own strengths, preferences, opinions, experiences, knowledge, beliefs, etc. to the table to help create a shared vision. As a result, each owns 50 percent of the company and owns 50 percent of the voting rights.

This is a partnership, so the two of you are a team with one goal in mind—to successfully (and happily) manage this company throughout the rest of your life. And, as partners, not only do you each have an equal ownership, you also have an equal **duty**—complete with a job description—to undertake, contribute, and complete your 50 percent. Notice, that's not 49 percent vs. 51 percent, or 51 percent vs. 49 percent; it's a true 50/50 split, and it's important to keep the balance of power just that—balanced!

Passively ignoring your responsibility or aggressively taking on more than your fair share will lead to hurt, anger, distrust, and confusion in meeting your goals. This is where taking an active and equal role in voting becomes important. By passively allowing your partner to decide for you or define your role, you are not holding up your end of the marriage deal. Have you ever said or thought:

- I just don't care, you decide.
- I want (my partner) to pick.
- I don't know.
- I'm afraid (my partner) will get upset.
- It doesn't matter what I think.
- It doesn't matter anymore, I give up.
- I don't want a fight.

Or have you ever used the 'silent treatment' and refused to talk? If so, then you could be holding your partner responsible for something that is actually part of **your** job description: the safeguarding of your own happiness in your marriage. In other words, it's your job to make sure you are pleased with the development and direction of the 'family business'—your relationship. That's what it means to take ownership.

Similarly, you are accountable for conflicts that occur when you arbitrarily override your partner, or independently make decisions about the way your role and your partner's role "should" be carried out. Have you ever said or thought:

- It's easier (or faster) if you just let me take care of it.
- This really is the only way we can do it.
- I don't see why you care so much about this.
- I don't think we have any other options here.
- I'm really good at this stuff, why don't we just let me handle it?

This kind of taking over when it comes to decision making is just as problematic as neglecting to step up to the plate. Grabbing onto power that is not yours can be a subtly manipulative move or a more aggressive, demanding kind of action. Regardless of your style, insisting on doing things your way is just as much of a roadblock for a healthy relationship as the abdication of responsibility described above. Remember, you are business owners who actively, responsibly, and jointly vote, 50/50, on decisions for the good of the marriage.

And, because you each bring your own definitions of marriage to the partnership, you may have many differences of opinion that could easily escalate into arguments. In the design and building of your partnership consider taking these steps:

1. Create a motivating and positive environment by encouraging each other to excel in your respective work, and move forward.

2. Base your partnership on honesty, trust, mutual respect, recognition of each other, and support.

3. Decide how much time, energy, and effort is needed. How much are you willing to contribute? Someone happy with a 'bare bones' marriage will not see the need for as much investment in these areas as someone who may be expecting the marriage to make up the bulk of his or her satisfaction with life.

4. Clearly define your job descriptions which can be created through a division of chores. If you have trouble starting, consider the responsibilities of overseeing finances, home management and house cleaning, spiritual needs, career goals, personal health and development needs, recreational pursuits, and family activities as potential items for your list of identified chores.

5. Base your job duties on the strengths and limitations of each partner. For example, one of you may be good at finances while the other is better at home maintenance. Draw on each person's knowledge, experience, intuition, and business sense when setting the course you will take together. Decide when the one taking responsibility for a specific area should have the authority to make decisions and choices, remembering to build in room for flexibility as well. Understand, however, that this is never about generating some kind of power struggle; rather it is about creating an efficient and effective system for handling life's tasks. At some point, you might want to consider doing some cross-training in various areas (e.g., finances) to safeguard against running into unexpected problems or having the power differential in a certain area become too lopsided.

Business owners take seriously the task of deciding who will do what to keep the business going and growing. With each of you committing to contribute an equivalent amount of time, energy, and effort, any division of labor that fits you as partners will work, as long as you both agree on the contributions required from each of you. There needs to be a mutuality in both commitment level and workload in order for you to maintain a balanced relationship.

Achieving such a balance can be a challenge, however. Personal, societal, and gender expectations all impact how couples look at sharing power and responsibility in their marriage. Many couples have ideas about sharing

Roommates, Not Partners

Tim and Nancy married two years ago, but have recently discussed getting a divorce on several occasions. They state they have difficulty talking to each other and are experiencing problems with trust. When asked why they got married in the first place, they each say "I don't know." Not only do they not know what they want from their marriage, they haven't actually worked together as a couple on anything since planning their wedding, and they haven't considered the option of doing so in preparing for their future, either. In a sense, they are co-existing in the same house, saying "We're both independent and each of us likes to do things our own way." They have no structure, no agreement, no real partnership. They have not yet made a start at building or developing a life together.

ownership in their marriage that are wildly different. One husband attending therapy thought his half of joint ownership in the marriage was made up of making the financial decisions (since he was earning the money) and his wife's half involved getting to decorate (and clean) the house. The wife in another client couple described her contribution to the marriage as returning to school and continuing to pursue her passion for playing competitive tennis. Her stymied and frustrated husband could not understand where the money was going to come from, how their home was going to be managed, and just what her role in managing the partnership business was going to be.

Because of these differences, several exercises are provided below to help you assess the effectiveness of your working relationship. You can use any or all of them to check whether you have a problem with ownership in your marriage. Just be sure you don't avoid or neglect this step, it is a crucial part of creating the foundation on which you will be building later.

Exercise #1: Exploring what has already been accomplished

1. At what point during your relationship did you view yourselves as partners?
2. When considering marriage, did you both discuss a common vision (e.g., hopes, dreams, goals) of how your marriage would evolve? Were you in clear agreement on these? What about an agreed-upon definition of ownership as it applies to marriage? If this was worked out between you at one time, are you still on board with that model definition now? (When asked, "What is the ownership arrangement in your marriage?" just about every couple comes out with two markedly different answers. There are always two different views of the contributions of each partner as well as their job descriptions, and a good deal of surprise at the extent of the differences!)
3. Have you discussed and agreed upon your individual contributions to the marriage as well as the job descriptions each will undertake?
4. Would you consider your marriage to be a 50/50 balanced partnership? What changes, if any, would you propose?
5. Does your environment encourage both partners to excel in their contributions to the marriage?

Exercise #2: Reaching for an objective perspective

Imagine yourself being hired as a consultant by you and your partner to help strengthen your team approach. What feedback would you offer to both the partnership and to each individual owner? What are each person's strengths and what skills would you suggest need improvement?

Exercise #3: Identifying different perspectives

Take some time to write down a sentence or two in response to each term or phrase on the list below, then share what you have written with each other. The purpose of this exercise is to clarify how each of you sees your marriage as it appears through the lens of a business model application, so don't be surprised or concerned to find differences in perspective and in your approach to answering these terms.

- Ownership in a marriage
- Partners are equal
- Contributions of each to the marriage
- Job descriptions of each partner
- Underlying vision for the marriage
- Current plan of action
- Equal voting by each partner
- Management style of each partner
- Shared roles for each partner
- Equal division of duties by each partner

Exercise #4: Standing together on common ground

So just how different are your ideas of "a joint partnership"—the phrase we started with at the beginning of this section? If you are in agreement on how you share your 50/50 ownership at this point, congratulations! Feel free to move on to the next section.

If you have some issues to work through before you can come to a solid agreement, then try working together to compile a joint list of duties, chores, etc. that have not yet been addressed. Keep the list available and add to it when either of you discovers areas of your relationship that are problematic. The goal here is to find out where you are in agreement about how to be in joint partnership with each other. All this discussing, understanding, and agreeing upon what it means to be owners is meant to give your marriage the same kind of clarity that business owners enjoy in their business partnerships. How ironic that it is easier to achieve a realistic, concrete agreement when talking about owning a business such as a gift shop or a sports bar with someone, than when talking about how we want to be married to the person we love! Let's bring that transparency and specificity into the marriage partnership as well.

By now, you should have in place a shared commitment to managing your marriage that involves a mutual understanding of what it means to be joint 50/50 owners of the family business. Now it's time to move on to the second aspect of your commitment statement, identifying your vision and plan.

With a Vision and a Plan

In the business world, company mergers occur on a regular basis and these require both a vision and a design plan to fuse two existing entities into one. A clear description of the vision of the new company, along with a comprehensive plan of action, decreases stress and conflict, conserves time and energy, and expedites the evolution of a fully functioning new organization.

Your marriage has also been a merger of sorts, meshing two individual lives into one successful and smoothly operating relationship. Developing your marriage begins with a unified vision of the entity you are going to build.

Let's suppose you decide to start a business with someone. You form a partnership and invest every resource you own in that business. You draw up and sign all the legal documents and begin to feel excited about getting your business up and running! But before that can happen, you'll need to nail down exactly how you want your business to look and operate. Let's say it's a restaurant you're opening. What's on the menu? How many staff will be hired and who will do the hiring? What hours will each person work? What will the job descriptions involve? What about staff training? And finances? Policies and procedures? Who orders supplies? These are just a few of the many questions you will need to answer before you first open the doors.

We can apply this business scenario to something a bit more relevant to your relationship. How about the plans you and your spouse made for your wedding? Some weddings are very simple and others are quite elaborate. As a couple, how was your wedding design chosen and who implemented the plans? How were those decisions made? How were tasks delegated? Were you happy with the teamwork and the outcome?

Now think back to your decision to marry. You probably had a picture in your head about what marriage would be like. The variation in these expectations is endless—anything from a cozy family in a little house with a white picket fence to a dual-career couple living in a downtown high-rise. How does the picture you held in your heart during your engagement compare with your current reality? If today you were able to create your ideal marriage, what would that ideal look like? Compare your vision of that ideal with your partner's vision, and take note of where they are similar and where they differ. Are there any surprises?

Your goal as a couple is to come up with one agreed-upon vision, and this is an important step. Can you imagine what it would be like to work for a company that expects employees to meet opposing goals? Living in a marriage with conflicting expectations is just as difficult.

A Vision But No Joint Plan

Diana and Steve's marriage reached a crisis point when Diana, having stayed at home to care for their son, stated that she was bored and ready to resume her career in marketing. Steve was ready to add more children to the family and admitted he saw Diana's role in the marriage as being a traditional stay-at-home mom. He was against her pursuing her career; she refused to discuss having more children until their differences were resolved. It seems that both of them had assumed—rather than discussed—the kind of 'business' they were planning and building together. They had a vision for their marriage, and that was to be happy and enjoy life. But they had not taken the next step of working through the important mechanics of joint ownership that are crucial in any marriage, just as they are in business. Unfortunately, when they began this work, they discovered the action plans they each had developed to guide their progress as a family were distinctly different.

In working together on this goal, just about any relationship you design will represent a 50/50 partnership because **you both will be agreeing to a shared vision and plan for your marriage**. The visions and plans that are truly shared do not and will not move forward without the consenting vote of both owners!

Once you have generated a single shared vision, the next step is to translate it into action by creating a working plan together. This plan should be designed to make things happen, to strengthen and solidify your partnership, and to help you achieve your goals as you move forward into the future.

Here are some concrete tips for designing your plan of action:

1. As you design your plan, make sure your steps move you forward at a speed that allows you to see progress; if you dawdle along too slowly, you may become discouraged.
2. Be discerning about what is important and what is not; while grand ideas are key, don't forget the many smaller

points. Set priorities—you don't want to be planning forever!

3. Focus on **contributing**, not on **critiquing** your partner's
   contributions.
4. Be sure you include discussion on the division of chores.
   Nailing down an effective way of consistently taking care
   of these responsibilities is essential to the success of any
   company or relationship.
5. Brainstorm often and be innovative in finding steps forward.
6. When planning, write down a description of your ideal
   marital vision and refer to it often.
7. Don't take a backseat to your partner. The success of
   fulfilling your ideal vision requires both of you to act as
   visionaries.
8. While planning is certainly work, forget perfectionism
   and remember to have fun!
9. Set specific meetings for specific topics; for example, make
   your vision the focus for one session, cover strategizing at
   another, and plan operational tasks at a third.
10. Continually look for those things that are in the best inter-
    est of the marriage; keep this idea current.

Policies and Procedures

Along with a defined vision and a plan of action to ensure that
vision is realized, any well-run company has policies and procedures
which provide a foundation for supporting the vision and plan. Policies are general guidelines that are relied upon when making major
decisions and determining a course of action as the company moves
forward. Examples include policies that cover legal and govern-

mental requirements, environmental concerns, and staff development. Procedures clarify, in more specific terms, the steps required
to smoothly and consistently adhere to the policies and support the
overall success of the company.

In a well-balanced marriage, partners working from an agreed-
upon vision and plan of action focus on some combination of the
following categories of daily living to provide a foundation and
structure for their relationship: financial stability; home management; career and professional goals; physical, emotional, and spiritual well-being; personal development; family health; community
service; and recreational and leisure activities. Those couples with
children would include parenting practices in their list as well.

Depending on the categories you select to form a foundation for
your marriage, you can create your own general policies and stipulate
as many or as few specific procedures as needed. For example, suppose you choose financial stability, career and professional goals, and
recreational and leisure activities as important features in the vision
for your marriage. Turning each of these into policies and generating
a few accompanying procedures might look something like this:

Financial stability

In order to maintain adequate income for covering all expenses and
contributing to saving for future goals (e.g., buying a house, retire-
ment, yearly vacations, etc.), we both agree to:

1. Limit eating out at restaurants to one time per week.
2. Discuss and agree before making major purchases.
3. Adhere to and support our budget for home expenses.

Career and professional goals

In order to help both of us pursue and fulfill our career aspirations
(e.g., finish college coursework, advance on a path of continued
intellectual and personal satisfaction, etc.), we both agree to:

1. Finance college expenses until both of us have finished our degree requirements.
2. Discuss our career goals before making major changes.
3. Support each other in reaching our individual academic and career goals.

Recreational and leisure activities

In order to be able to afford pleasurable activities, small and large, on an ongoing basis, we both agree to:

1. Save for one major vacation each year; the maximum amount to be spent will be agreed upon six weeks in advance of our departure.
2. Go out together at least once a month for a 'date night.'
3. Provide input on activities that we would like to share with each other.

Keep in mind that all this work doesn't have to be done overnight. These are concrete exercises to use as resources throughout your whole journey. Consider your endeavors in this area to be a work in progress, as policies will have to be updated through the years and procedures will need to be added or modified to fit the policies. An effective process for designing your policies and procedures is outlined in the steps below:

1. From the box above, select the categories of daily living that best encompass the goals for your marital vision. In a well-balanced relationship, partners typically choose many, if not all, of the categories listed.
2. For each category chosen, brainstorm ways to describe how that category is of value to your marriage and what goals you want to achieve. This can help you finalize how you want to state your policies in written form.

Categories of Daily Living

Financial stability

Relationship development
(marriage)

Home management

Family health

Career and professional goals

Recreational and leisure activities

Physical, emotional, spiritual well-being

Personal interests

Parenting practices

3. Then develop a list of specific ways you can contribute to the goals of each policy and rank them in terms of relevance, importance, and ease of achievement.
4. Discuss how each policy will support and ensure that your vision is on course.
5. Identify and list any areas of confusion or disagreement. You can create a procedure to be placed within a troubling policy that will help eliminate problem issues.
6. Have a document listing your policies and procedures handy so you can refer to them when needed; keep it up to date with the changes in your marriage.

Board Meetings

Just as business executives meet to make decisions and come up with plans for the future, you and your spouse, as executive family members, will need to hold regular and productive board meetings to hammer out solutions to problems and agree on strategies for moving your business forward. In the process, you will need to communicate a great deal of information, but you are not meeting simply to trade perspectives or to argue and coerce. Your main objective is to achieve consensus.

Business people who dread attending meetings have been subjected to too much disorganization and ineffective use of time. Sometimes there are no clearly stated goals and a few participants are allowed to dominate a meeting while others sit passively without contributing. This is not the kind of board meeting you want to hold! Yours will be active, energized, and organized. It will serve as a time for productive communication, problem-solving, and clear thinking. The agenda will include discussion that:

- Improves the routine of your partnership.
- Advances progress toward your shared goals.
- Addresses disruptions, threats, or complications.
- Reports on new developments, additions, and successes.

Certainly a professional and adult approach is required, meaning you will need to take responsibility for your actions, feelings, and the decisions made both at the meeting and afterward as you carry out the tasks you agreed to undertake. Here is a step-by-step approach for holding a productive board meeting:

Preparation:

- Make an agenda—a list of issues you need to discuss.
- Write down your thoughts and suggestions for each one.
- Collect and bring with you information and papers needed to work on the issues.
- Pick a time and place convenient for both of you and conducive to focused work.

Attitude:

- Keep a positive outlook.
- Head in a constructive, not a destructive, direction.
- Work to move things forward.

- Be prepared for conflict but don't let it become the focus of your meeting.

During the meeting:

- Set time limits for each topic.
- Defer extended discussions until the end of the meeting, after other issues are resolved.
- If you can't come to an agreement on a difficult topic, table the discussion knowing you've at least made some progress.

When you've finished, congratulate yourselves on a job well done, recognize the progress you've made on important and difficult issues, and go on to enjoy life together outside the boardroom!

While you are meeting, stay with your logical, rational side as you work through problem-solving and task planning. You will also need to tap into some creative thinking as you search for alternative solutions to a variety of issues. Theoretically, there are an unlimited number of options along the continuum between your position and your partner's. Just as there are endless shades of gray between black and white, there are endless possibilities for compromise as the two of you search for a point of agreement. You just need to make the decision that you **will** choose one of the many solutions you come up with in your problem-solving work.

Voting is the vehicle by which you will act to resolve each issue during board meetings. This can be challenging, since each of you owns exactly 50 percent of the company and therefore will have precisely 50 percent of the voting power. However, you can do a lot to avoid potential deadlocks by designing solutions that meet both your needs, making it relatively easy to agree and vote the same way. Also, think back to the points discussed in the section on partnership above, and the exercises you worked through to identify your own shared vision of partnership in marriage. Voting is one place where this vision is translated into reality. That's why it's important to vote in a straightforward manner, even when you feel pulled to cast your vote in your partner's best interest instead of your own. As an occasional occurrence, this can be a kind, self-sacrificial, and sometimes even heroic action, but if it's an ongoing pattern of self-denial or submission, it can undermine the voting process. At the same time, pushing too hard for the vote to fall in your own favor without regard for your partner's ideas may demonstrate a self-centered and aggressive position that can yield negative consequences.

Negotiation and Compromise

Rarely is business conducted without the use of negotiation. Likewise, few marriages survive a serious lack of negotiating ability on the part of the spouses involved. Knowing how to negotiate is essential to developing a rewarding relationship and reaching your goals.

Take time to think through the points you will be discussing and develop a well-considered position for each issue. That way you'll have a structured, organized plan for proceeding with your negotiations. Then spend some time contemplating the big picture as well. Can you name your reasons for entering into negotiation on a given topic? What are your overall goals for the outcome? How are they of value to the marriage vision and plan? Your positions should be truly fair, equitable, and reasonable for **both** of you. If they're not, you have more work to do.

Power Plays

- Talking down to the other person
- Interrupting
- Using intimidation tactics

Power Give-Aways

- Failing to offer input or suggestions
- Not preparing well enough
- Giving up, giving in

Going through this process will help you think through what it is you really want to gain through negotiation. Compromise costs, so it's important that you ask your spouse to sacrifice only when necessary in order to resolve an issue of great significance to you. Consider what your partner is going to have to give up, and make sure it's for a higher purpose—and for the marriage, not just so you can have your own way.

After preparing what you will say, you must also prepare yourself to listen and really hear your partner. Understand you are going to hear the word "NO!" and decide on some strategies for dealing with this, along with a back-up plan should your first choices prove untenable. You will need to come to the table with flexibility built into both your negotiation plan and your attitude.

Also, realize that you might be the one saying "NO!" at some point. When this happens, understand this can't be your final word on the subject. Follow it up with an idea for moving the process forward by offering a reasonable alternative. This allows you to have input into the eventual solution, giving you some say in the creation of the option you will both eventually agree upon.

Some issues don't allow a compromise. If your spouse gets a promotion that requires a cross-country move to Los Angeles, but you want to stay near family in New York, deciding to live half-way between in St. Louis is not going to help. In such cases, you can always choose to take turns; this time, you win and the family stays put, but next time (and there will be a next time!) your spouse gets the deciding vote on a major life issue. Other issues may be better resolved by agreeing to disagree. If arriving late for appointments drives you up a wall while your spouse hates wasting five minutes waiting, you may need to choose to drive separately to some of the more important appointments or events on your calendar so each of you can stay within your comfort zone.

And, don't forget: if you reach an impasse during your negotiations, you can always take a break, rethink the important points, brainstorm more options, and try again at a later date.

Self Check:
What's Your Motivation?

Are you finding it impossible to think of different ways to solve a problem? Do you keep turning aside possible solutions? Refuse to give a little in order to get a little? Maybe you aren't really invested in the negotiation process, you're simply looking for a way to gain the upper hand. If you're in this to win, then you're playing a whole different game. Negotiation is about compromise, and the definition of compromise is when everyone goes away a little unhappy—each of you gets some of what you want, but not all.

Communication

The most basic rule of effective communication is to make sure you listen more than you speak. In both business and marriage, you can't consider yourself a good communicator unless you know how to really listen to others. Communication experts call this active listening, and a few foundational precepts are:

1. Use open-ended questions to explore your partner's thoughts and ideas. Say "What do you think about this option?" rather than "Do you like this solution or not?" The latter question allows a yes-or-no response which will not tell you nearly as much as an answer to the former question which requires more complex information.
2. Paraphrase what you hear your partner say as a way of checking to see if you are both on the same page. Be careful not to simply repeat the same words, which can come off as patronizing and dismissive. Use your own language to describe what your partner has shared.
3. Make sure your nonverbal communication is respectful and attentive. Factors such as eye contact and body posture can contradict and even overrule what your words are

saying, so take care to send the same message through all modes of communication.

What does good communication sound like? It contains a lot of straight talk, and an equal amount of good listening. Questions are asked, clarifications are made, and it's obvious that each participant is trying to see things from the other's point of view. The focus is on sharing information, exploring options and solving problems. The back-and-forth flow is consistent, with no one person dominating the conversation.

> ## Quick Tips for Straight Talk
> - Stay focused
> - Stick to the subject
> - Keep on track
> - No emotional venting
> - Don't give up

Disruptions in the communication process can happen from time to time. Take an active role in sorting them out to avoid unnecessary roadblocks. One key issue is emotional reactivity. Are emotions getting in the way of problem-solving? Have you somehow shifted gears from logical processing into expressing your feelings? If so, consider the best way to get back on track. Can you simply stop, reverse, and go back to dealing with the issue at hand using a cognitive approach? If this isn't appropriate, try setting aside 5-10 minutes to briefly process your feelings with the idea of reducing the emotional intensity so you can get back to work.

Other communication problems may stem from power issues in your relationship. Any equal partnership needs to be characterized by mutual respect and a caring attitude. Handling conflict well is a big part of this, and it is crucial that you refrain from expressing disagreement as criticism. Avoid equating 'different' with 'wrong', as in labeling your partner's ideas, preferences, solutions, or priorities as wrong because they are different from your own. If you find yourself criticizing instead of looking for common ground, maybe you are grasping for power that doesn't belong to you. It could be you are trying to tell your partner how to think or act—something you don't actually have control over—rather than taking care of your own business, which in reality is all that you have the power to do something about.

'I' sentences are very handy tools in such situations. For example, "I feel so defeated when you say things never change," is a non-critical way of communicating your perspective to your partner, whereas "You make me feel awful," is not. Similarly, "I felt pretty intimidated when you just said we have to do this your way, or else," trumps "You think you know everything" any day.

Another potential landmine is the use of 'always' and 'never.' These words, when used to describe someone else's actions, paint that person with broad strokes of negative color and are guaranteed to escalate the conflict. The conversation suddenly goes from "How can we figure out a relatively painless way to get the kids to school on time all the time?" to "You are always late" and "You never help enough in the mornings." You'll find that you can express yourself completely during a disagreement without using 'always' and 'never', and have a much better chance of finding common ground when you avoid them.

During your discussions about how to run the family business, think about how you would proceed in a business environment. What kinds of limits would there be on your input into a business colleague's behavior? Most likely, you could address problems and suggest changes, but if these communications are rebuffed, you'd need to be able to move the business at hand forward in a positive and professional way in spite of the difficulties you experience. Use these same expectations as a guide for communicating in your marriage, and see how far they take you.

So are you feeling like a team now? After all your hard work, you should be! The next step is to delve into Part II to learn more about your emotional relationship and how it will interface with the business management skills introduced in this first section.

Communication Do's and Don'ts

- DO stay focused, stick to the topic.
- DO listen carefully and respectfully.
- DO respond empathically; try to see the other's point of view.
- DO use 'I' sentences instead of 'You' sentences.
- DO take a time out if there is a breakdown in communications.
- DO stick with the facts instead of mere opinion.

Are you serious about coming to a resolution to the issue at hand? Then DON'T give up.

- DON'T try to win or be right—power plays are damaging.
- DON'T interrupt, it's disrespectful toward your partner.
- DON'T resort to giving anyone the silent treatment.
- DON'T mind-read, blame, keep score, get defensive, sit passively, or become aggressive.
- DON'T label, call names, or use any of the following words: should, ought, always, or never.

PART II

And Now... The Feelings

So, with the *Marriage is a Business* approach, it should be easy to turn any troubled marriage around, right? And it should be easy for any new couple to get off to a great start, too, by designing and developing their marriage along business guidelines, right?

Well, not exactly! There's more to love and marriage than the business end of the deal. Don't forget the whole emotional side of a relationship, where things can and do get tricky. Managing feelings can be quite different from dealing in thoughts and ideas, and often

---

Key Points from Part I

As we begin now to examine the role of feelings in a relationship, it is important not to forget or put aside what was previously discussed. In Part I, we looked at a business model to logically define, design, and implement a structure that can help stabilize marriages. Marriage is a business. It has:

- Two owners
- A single shared vision
- A working business plan
- Defined policies and procedures

- Scheduled board meetings
- A corporate culture involving skillful communication, negotiation, and compromise

---

it's the emotional part of human nature that creates problems—and thus disconnection or conflict—in our relationships. When couples enter therapy, they do so primarily because they're **feeling** bad (usually sad, mad, or scared) and so the emotional side of their relationship must be addressed and managed, along with the business side of marriage. The emotional factors within a relationship then mesh with the intellectual, objective, business factors and this mix strengthens, deepens, and enriches a marriage.

The world of feelings doesn't have to be a big mystery. This section of the book will explain the world of feelings and:

- Enable you to notice your feelings, know your feelings, and own your feelings.
- Help you learn to manage your feelings rather than have them manage you.
- Teach you how to use your feelings to help you make better decisions and choices.
- Explain how to balance your feelings in relation to your partner (and others).

Entering the World of Feelings

Psychologically, we as individuals operate on both intellectual (thoughts) and emotional (feelings) levels. By the time we reach adulthood, we have begun to integrate our thoughts and feelings. Most of us—but some more than others—have developed an identity at this stage, an operating sense of who we are, how we are, what we like and dislike, want or don't want, believe in or reject. We are likely to have generated specific expectations, visions, and goals based on this identity and each of us proceeds to go through our adult years intellectually designing and leading a life based on these facets.

If we look at this from a business point of view once again, it could be said that a person comes into adulthood as a sole proprietor—a business owner with a vision to design and enjoy life. We are all working our individual plans and developing our own policies and procedures. Intellectually, we are each in charge of and responsible for the quality of life we create for ourselves. And the stronger and more fully developed this quality of life is, the more we are able to contribute to a marriage partnership.

> **Marriage**
>
> Coming together involves three key responsibilities:
>
> - Both partners intellectually manage the vision and the plan for the relationship
> - Each partner intellectually manages his/her own vision and plan (to be blended with the partnership vision)
> - Each partner intellectually manages his/her own feelings

As sole proprietors, each of us is also intellectually in charge of and responsible for managing our own feelings. That is to say, as a company of one, each of us is responsible for our own happiness, sadness, anger, and fear. The success we achieve in leading emotionally satisfying lives depends on how well we, as owners/managers, oversee the ongoing emotional operations of our individual lives. And, as a relationship grows, it becomes more and more important over time that each partner intellectually sees, knows, and owns his or her own feelings so that a successful blending of two lives can take place.

A marriage of two lives (a merger of two sole proprietorships) can be emotionally trying as each person aligns his or her own vision alongside that of their partner and both work toward carrying out a single, unified marital plan. Throughout their marriage, both partners will be challenged with finding a way not only to stay true to themselves and their own identities, but also to accommodate and blend with each other to form a close, loving, and lasting bond.

"So, I'm supposed to manage—not control—my own feelings?"

Yes, and more specifically, you are supposed to use your thoughts to manage your feelings. Years of psychological research have taught us a lot about the ways in which thoughts can generate and intensify emotions. One common finding has to do with how people explain to themselves why things happen—how they interpret the causes of events in their lives. In other words, **what you think** about the causes of specific events can impact **how you feel** about them. Here's a simple diagram showing how this works:

situation ⟶ thought ⟶ feeling
rainy weather ⟶ good for the yard ⟶ happy
rainy weather ⟶ ruined plans ⟶ unhappy

Emotional self-management implies overseeing your feelings, and being aware of and using options for resolving feelings that can sabotage the quality of your personal life and your relationship. Your thoughts are key to accomplishing this effectively.

Keeping with the simple approach illustrated in the diagram above, let's look at thoughts as being separated into two types: negative thoughts and positive thoughts. Negative thoughts can be described as being irrational, self-defeating, destructive, or nonproductive and may limit you by implying you can't, shouldn't, won't, must, must not, etc. On the other hand, positive thoughts are rational, constructive, or productive, and represent more accurately what you believe, choose, and consider to be healthy. Overall, these thoughts are a representation of who you are and your view of life.

Below are a few case studies showing how issues of emotional self-management can manifest themselves in relationships.

AND NOW... THE FEELINGS

Case Study: Keith didn't know how to manage his feelings.

Having grown up leading a charmed life, Keith's early relationships were anything but charmed. In each one, he came to interpret his role as that of a rescuer of women. This role required him to be accommodating and tolerant of behavior that he didn't like while holding back on expressing his own needs and desires. He has replicated this pattern in his current marriage and is depressed, withdrawn, and distant from his wife.

Choosing which thoughts to attend to will influence greatly how you feel. Listening to negative thoughts will generate negative feelings; listening to positive thoughts will elicit more positive feelings. By being aware of this thought-feeling connection, you are in a position to decide whether or not you will do something to change. If, for instance, you are feeling sad and can identify the thoughts that create that sadness, then you are in a position to change those thoughts and thus decrease or resolve your sadness.

Just as it takes knowledge and practice to own and manage a business—including the business of marriage—emotional self-management must be learned and practiced. It does not happen naturally. Therefore, you have to choose to take responsibility for learning and practicing emotional self-management. There are many tools that can help you handle this responsibility successfully. Throughout this book you will find several lists containing exercises and advice, as well as boxes containing practical tips. Together, these points make up our Partnership Tools which you will find organized into a handy summarized format at the back of the book.

Managing your feelings means **you** yourself **choose** to take charge of how you feel and how you will act in response to your feel-

ings—in other words, your behavior. These days, people are too apt
to make excuses or blame others for making them sad, upset, nervous, depressed, or—most notably—angry. While it certainly makes
good sense to recognize the connection between others' behaviors
and your own emotions, it is important to understand that just
because there is a **connection**, as in, "I feel anxious when you drive
this fast," does not mean you are trapped into behaving a certain
way, or living with a certain feeling if it is uncomfortable for you.
What you decide to do in reaction to another's actions is really up to
you, and you alone are in control of that decision. It is important to
accept that, as an adult partner in a relationship**, you must choose
to take responsibility for attending to and managing the feelings you generate across all situations.** Thus, a person who feels
anxious because of a partner's choices or behavior does not have to
act anxiously or stay stuck in the anxiety; there are other options
which are more empowering, constructive, and emotionally healthy.

What was happening with Keith?

- If Keith ever had a personal vision for his life, he has
  chosen to prioritize the plans of others and forgotten to
  address his own.
- Keith has not taken responsibility for addressing and
  managing the emotional difficulties this self-neglect has
  created for him.
- It does not appear that Keith has done the necessary
  work of agreeing upon and supporting a joint relationship plan.

Case Study: Debbie didn't keep up with managing and communicating about her feelings.

Debbie seems relatively satisfied with the financial plans she and her husband have agreed upon. They both oversee their own money and support the marriage partnership by contributing toward joint goals for the future. However, Debbie's husband recently purchased an expensive car without consulting her and she found herself stuck in the resentment and hurt that she experienced as a result. Debbie was able to recognize that she wanted the opportunity to express her opinion and stay informed about this expensive decision (she saw it as related to their joint future goals). But she decided these emotions were her husband's problem, not hers—after all, it was his fault she felt this way. As the couple processed through this issue, Debbie was surprised to learn this dream car represented a lifetime achievement for her husband, as he had never shared this information with her.

Managing your feelings also implies that **you choose to consistently oversee** your feelings and prevent them from taking charge over you. Emotional self-management is not something you do one time or once a day. It's a skill acquired over a lifetime that can become routine. With any life change, no matter how small, there is a corresponding emotional change. The more significant the change in your life, the stronger your emotional change is likely to be. If your feelings change in a negative direction, chances are you will feel a need to do something. The choices you make as a result make up the bulk of managing your feelings. These choices can range anywhere from denying there is a problem to letting your feelings overwhelm you to the point of losing control. Operating at such extremes is not helpful and there are a lot of positive, emotionally healthy options in between.

What was happening with Debbie?

- Debbie (and her husband) were relatively clear regarding their own visions for their lives; both reported being happy with themselves and the marriage.
- Debbie was aware of her feelings of hurt and apprehension, but didn't know what to do with them. Instead, she wanted her husband to read her mind, change his behavior accordingly, and ultimately remedy how she felt.
- While the couple had a general financial plan in place, developing their policies more fully could help address specific situations such as this one as their marriage progresses.
- Rather than getting lost in her emotions, Debbie needed to take responsibility for attending to and managing her hurt feelings. She needed to call a board meeting to propose options for change. Her husband, like the rest of us, is not a mind-reader!

Case Study: Ron controlled his wife instead of managing his feelings.

Ron loves life. He loves his wife and son, his job, and his friends. He feels truly fortunate and wants all this to continue. He's also fearful all this will go away. So fearful, in fact, that he tries to control situations, e.g., his relationship with his wife, as much as is humanly possible. Feeling burdened by his micromanaging, Ron's wife disengages, consults with family members, or passively tolerates his manipulation. All this makes her question the strength of their marriage, however, and as Ron's anxiety builds and his micromanaging increases in response to her doubts, a destructive cycle has been created.

Notice there is a big difference between **managing** and **controlling** your feelings. The idea is not to force your emotions to fit into some kind of preconceived mold or rigid ideal. Denying, discounting, or ignoring your feelings in an effort to control them will not lead to a healthy emotional life in the long run. Instead, healthy relationships are built on first accepting feelings as real and valid and then managing them effectively in order to make constructive decisions about what to do next. This difference between 'managing' and 'controlling' is well known to business professionals who manage a team of employees. Good leaders know the difference between managing their staff and trying to control them. They don't deny, discount, or ignore the assets of their employees, but they don't let their staff's shortcomings ruin the company's chances for success, either.

The workplace is actually a prime environment for observing how people learn to manage their feelings, as most employees have mastered this challenge in order to make a good impression and advance their careers. Who wants to have a meltdown in a staff meeting, or lose his or her temper with a coworker in front of the boss? Similarly, just about everyone has learned to manage difficult feelings in public places. What happens when a diner gets a piece of bad news while having a meal at a restaurant or when a driver is given an expensive speeding ticket by a highway patrol officer? In the vast majority of cases, strong or difficult emotions are handled appropriately in public or in the presence of authority figures, and this means feelings are being effectively managed. Because they have an intellectual awareness of what is appropriate, as well as an awareness of their own emotional reaction, these people are able to choose behavioral options that:

- Address the situation at hand.
- Reflect their emotional experience.
- Are in keeping with their own best interests.

If such constructive choices are made every day in work and public contexts, it is certainly possible to carry them out in more private situations. Think of how this applies to you and your spouse in your marriage: **If you have successfully made suitable choices in dealing with your feelings on the job, in public situations, and in front of authority figures, you certainly can learn to do the same at home with your partner!**

What was happening with Ron?

- Ron is happy with his plan. His wife cannot identify her plan, and is not comfortable designing one.
- Neither Ron nor his wife have an awareness of their own feelings that is comprehensive enough to be useful. Both are unaware of the importance of choosing to manage their feelings. As a result, their feelings dictate their relationship.
- This couple has not done the work of choosing and agreeing upon a vision and plan for their marriage. Ron is using his own personal plan; his wife has not contributed her intellectual vision of the marital plan.

"But why do I have to do all this work?"

First of all, emotional self-management doesn't have to be difficult work; it's just a different kind of work. And if self-management skills were studied and learned during childhood like history, math, and science, we would not find them hard work at all. Unfortunately, emotional health is not taught in schools—or even in many homes—although it certainly needs to be. As children, we're expected to behave, but we are not taught how this relates to emotional self-management. And how can children successfully behave when their feelings are dictating their behavior? Generally, if children are taught at all about emotions, they are told to control, not manage, feelings. The opportunities for children to vent sadness and anger or to admit and address their fears vary greatly from family to family, but much of the time in our Western culture, they are absent. Additionally, even when these feelings are recognized, what options for constructively handling difficult emotions are taught to children as they grow? Consequently, people can enter adulthood (and adult relationships) without much of a clue about how to manage their feelings.

Add to this lack of early training the fact that humans operate on both an emotional and an intellectual level, and it is easy to see there is much room for confusion when communicating with others. Problems quickly show themselves when one individual starts talking on an intellectual level while a partner is hearing and responding from an emotional level. Like two ships passing in the night, they can totally miss each other's meaning and be left wondering, "What in the world just happened here? This conversation isn't even making sense!"

In addition to a lack of opportunity for learning about how to manage our emotions as we grow, once we reach adulthood we are often further discouraged from delving into the emotional realm. Societal expectations tend to keep us focused on our rational, thinking side and this leads us to suppress involvement with our emotional selves. In effect, our culture tells us, "If you are happy that's okay, but if you are sad, mad, or fearful then be sure you control (suppress) those feelings around other people."

Jeremy and Rebecca

It doesn't take long for Jeremy and Rebecca to start arguing. While they want their marriage to work and have tried countless times to resolve their differences, their discussions too easily slide from management issues to emotional sparring. Both are well educated professionals who excel in problem-solving and both are keenly aware of each other's emotional nuances. But whenever they disagree, without realizing what is happening they automatically shift their focus from management issues to feelings. Their discussing becomes arguing and they struggle to remember what the initial issue of concern was; they are not aware that feelings have become the topic of their argument. By reading and picking up emotional cues from each other during their debates, they start reacting emotionally rather than managing their feelings and staying intellectually focused on the management topic at hand.

As a result, they are learning to become pros at reacting, bickering, defending, blaming, shutting down, walking away, and giving up. Obviously this lack of personal emotional self-management is contributing little to ensure a smoothly managed marriage. Ultimately, both partners have become tired of trying, their marriage is more disappointing than fulfilling, and divorce has been considered.

"But I still don't understand why I have to manage my feelings!"

Many people ask why this kind of emotional insight and self-regulation doesn't happen naturally. After all, emotions are a natural phenomenon. While emotions are what make us humans unique, the fact is, management skills are not a natural phenomenon. Learning self-management skills is simply that—learning. In much the same way we learn about and work at good eating and exercise habits in order to maintain a healthy physical body even though our physical state is a 'natural' one, we must also educate and discipline ourselves with regards to our 'natural' feelings.

There are many excuses people use to deny or avoid learning emotional self-management. Have you ever thought to yourself, "Why can't I just be myself? I shouldn't have to go through all this when I get home from work. I just want to relax when I'm in my own home. If only my partner wouldn't… (fill in the blank!). My partner's behavior makes me feel so…(sad/mad/ scared)."

> If you choose not to learn, then you choose to keep emotional conflict in your life and accept the consequences that conflict can bring.

Well folks, the bottom line is that you are in the adult world now, and if you learn anything from this book (or from any other self-help book, for that matter), hopefully it will be that you and you alone are completely in charge of and responsible for your feelings. You assumed this responsibility, whether you wanted it or not, when you turned that magic age of 18. Welcome to adulthood! And regardless of whether or not you want this task, emotional self-management is your responsibility and duty. If you choose not to learn, then you choose to keep emotional conflict in your life and accept the consequences that conflict can bring.

You may not have been introduced to the concept of emotional self-management previously, but from now until the day you die, you and you alone will remain responsible for any emotional reaction you may have to the people, events, and circumstances throughout your life. Other people cannot **make** you feel anything. Your emotional reactions to others flow from what is inside you and are based on your intellectual interpretations; it is these interpretations that will determine, in part, the choices you make and the consequences of those choices.

And if you choose to accept this challenge to be emotionally in charge, remember that it's not necessarily hard work, just different work. Don't give up, but instead keep on choosing to do the work. Use your head (your thoughts), stay willing to learn, and study and practice. Don't get sidetracked by competing with, criticizing, or watching your partner's work, and don't think your partner has more work than you to do. As a new student, it is not your place to teach your partner; rather, your job is to become a master over your own emotional world!

Feelings Revealed

By now the point has been made that you are responsible for intellectually managing your feelings. But if you are like many people, you might be thinking, "I still don't get it. I don't know what it is I have to actually do." The emotional world can seem a bit of a mystery at times but it's not really that complicated.

Feelings can be classified into four general categories: happy, sad, mad, and scared. These categories can be further broken down into various levels of intensity such as low, medium, and high, or rated on a scale of 1 to 10. When emotional intensity is particularly high, an individual's rational side or judgment can sometimes become distorted or clouded. On the other hand, those who keep their emotional intensity deliberately low may not be able to identify how they feel at all, or may feel numbness rather than any specific emotion. Most of the countless moments of emotion you experience each day can be put into one of these four main groups. Confusing or hard-to-describe feelings can be recognized and understood based on the characteristics of the group to which they belong.

Take a look at the chart below. It includes an abbreviated list of feeling words that have been broken down by category and intensity. For example, words to describe anger range from mild frustration and irritation to intense fury and rage. Similarly, one can feel anywhere from blue and gloomy to downright depressed and empty, while fearfulness ranges from being apprehensive to petrified.

Just getting acquainted with the chart and using it creatively will significantly aid your ability to manage your feelings and understand the feelings of others, most particularly your partner. For example, you can:

1. Identify any feelings you've had today. Note the category and rate the intensity of each.
2. Spend time during the day noting the feelings of others around you, both at home and at work. As before, identify the category and rate the intensity for each.
3. Identify the feelings you most commonly experience. Would you describe yourself as typically happy, sad, mad, or scared? Can you offer explanations for the feelings you have?
4. Select one category (happy, sad, mad, or scared) and throughout the day identify people who exhibit that feeling.
5. Practice using feeling words in conversations, e.g., "I feel excited because I have great plans for the weekend," or "I feel nervous because I have a big exam tomorrow."
6. While listening to the conversations of others, identify any feeling words used.

Practicing some or all of these tasks will help you build your ability to identify feelings naturally and comfortably. This is crucial because in order to develop successful self-management skills, you must first know what it is you have to manage. Recognizing your emotions, being able to label them, and knowing when they are present will help you later determine management options that work best for you. Below are listed a wide variety of tools you can use for managing anger, anxiety, and sadness so you will always be able to develop the means to achieve self-management when the situation calls for it.

A Vocabulary of Feeling Words

INTENSITY	HAPPY	SAD	MAD	SCARED
LOW	Cheerful	Blue	Annoyed	Apprehensive
	Comfortable	Cheerless	Bugged	Disquieted
	Content	Disappointed	Cross	Fearful
	Glad	Doleful	Displeased	Fretful
	Pleased	Down	Frustrated	Nervous
	Satisfied	Downcast	Irked	Rattled
	Tickled	Dissatisfied	Irritated	Timid
		Low	Miffed	Unsure
			Peeved	Upset
			Ruffled	Uptight
MEDIUM	Blissful	Bereaved	Aggravated	Afraid
	Convivial	Dejected	Agitated	Alarmed
	Delighted	Distressed	Bitter	Anxious
	Gleeful	Forlorn	Cranky	Cowed
	Happy	Gloomy	Cross	Dreading
	Jolly	Glum	Disgruntled	Jittery
	Joyful	Hopeless	Disgusted	Panicked
	Joyous	Joyless	Mad	Scared
	Merry	Lugubrious	Nettled	Worried
	Upbeat	Melancholy	Rankled	
		Mournful	Resentful	
		Rueful	Riled	
		Sad		
		Somber		
		Sorrowful		
		Unhappy		
HIGH	Ecstatic	Anguished	Angry	Frantic
	Elated	Depressed	Enraged	Frightened
	Euphoric	Despairing	Fiery	Horrified
	Exhilarated	Despondent	Fuming	Overwrought
	Exultant	Devastated	Furious	Petrified
	Jubilant	Morose	Hateful	Terrified
	Overjoyed	Troubled	Incensed	
	Thrilled	Worthless	Inflamed	
			Infuriated	
			Irate	
			Livid	
			Outraged	

Anger

1. Plan for situations where you think your anger may surface. Remember the goal is not merely to survive the situation but to manage your anger using your thoughts.

   a. Have available a list of constructive thoughts to help you keep your focus on the discussion, and also on managing your emotions. For example,

      • Stay calm, nothing bad will happen.

      • Breathe!

      • This is not a battle; the other person has a right to his or her own opinion even though it may be different from mine.

      • I can walk away at any time; it's better to leave than let my anger get the best of me.

      • I can do this. I'm determined to manage my anger rather than let it manage me!

      • Let me step back and remember the topic at hand. What's the goal of this conversation after all?

      • I'm doing the best I can right now; I'm going to let the other person be responsible for doing his or her best, too.

   b. When speaking, start your sentences with "I". This allows you to own what you say and will increase your chances of not sounding defensive or confrontational. Try to eliminate sentences using "you", as these can put the other person in a defensive mode. Be aware of the other's use of "I" or "you" sentences, as this can help you understand any defensive feelings you may be experiencing as well.

   c. Remember the topic under discussion. Unless explicitly agreed upon, feelings are not the topic. When the focus shifts to feelings, then two topics are being discussed simultaneously; thus, conflict and confusion arise.

   d. Use a low-volume voice.

e. Use a 10-point scale to monitor the intensity of your angry feelings (see the Feelings Chart) and don't allow your feelings to get above a 5. The higher your intensity gets, the more likely those feelings will become unmanageable.

f. Monitor your physical signs of impending anger, such as a clenched jaw, clenched fists, defensive posture, muscle tension, facial tension, tight lips, shallow breathing, or pressure in your chest.

g. You can practice and learn (beforehand) what anger feels like in your body. The intensity of anger is contained within the confines of your body; it does not flow outside your body. If angry, try sitting down and watching how the anger swells, flows, then fades away. Once you can do this, you'll find it may not take too long before you'll come to a better vision of what it is that you have to manage. Since anger can seem all-consuming, knowing that it dissipates quickly may help you minimize the size of the problem it appears to create.

2. If your anger seems to be getting the best of you:

a. STOP and remove yourself from the situation.

b. Take a brisk walk or briefly engage in some other physical activity.

c. Breathe.

d. Focus on constructive statements and NOT on the statements that provoked your anger.

e. Write out your feelings or talk to a good, empathetic listener.

f. Try having the same discussion again, but only after your anger has dropped to a level that you rate no higher than 2 on a 10-point scale.

Anxiety

1. Plan for situations where you think your anxiety will surface. Know that your goal is anxiety management, not persevering through the situation while your nervousness builds to a panic.
2. Monitor your muscle tension and breathe deeply, slowly, and fully. Keeping oxygen flowing through your body will allow you to relax and focus on the situation at hand.
3. Have a list of constructive statements available. For example:
   - Take a deep breath, slow down, and relax.
   - No matter what happens, I know I'm doing my best right now.
   - My goal is to manage my nervousness, not stay in the situation.
   - If it helps, I can always leave and calm myself down.
   - I'm in charge of my feelings. I am going to keep breathing.
4. Know the signs of developing anxiety: tension, shallow breathing, faster heart beat, confused thoughts, sweaty palms, tight chest, etc.
5. Focus on managing the symptoms, not on the building anxiety. Focusing on the mounting anxiety or on trying to fight against the anxiety will only heighten it and make it more difficult to manage.
6. Get physically active; choose to take a walk, do chores or errands, or distract yourself with other activities that will help dissipate your anxiety.
7. Talk to a good, empathetic listener.
8. Try to identify the negative self-talk that generated the anxiety and change those thoughts to something more constructive or productive.

9. Practice assertiveness skills and learn your rights. Here are some assertive statements that can help:
   - I have the right to be treated fairly and with respect.
   - I have the right to my feelings, my beliefs, and my choices.
   - I have the right to feel safe and be in a safe environment.
   - I have the right to walk away if this is in my best interest.
   - I have the right to not be responsible for others' thoughts, beliefs, choices, or problems.
   - I have the right to say no and not feel guilty.

Sadness

1. Recognize your sadness and decide to change. If left unchecked, sadness can lead to depression. Common signs of depression include: difficulty sleeping, changes in appetite, loss of interest in activities, withdrawing from social activities, feelings of worthlessness, feelings of helplessness, frequent crying, and fatigue.
2. Get up and get going. Have a daily routine that keeps you occupied and busy. Too much free time allows your brain to get caught up in repeatedly replaying negative thoughts. Distract yourself from negative thoughts by doing chores, gardening, reading, or watching a movie.
3. Get out of your home and be around positive people, whether you interact with them or not.
4. Spend time in the sunlight.
5. Have a list of constructive thoughts to help steer you away from depression or sadness. For example:
   - I have options; there are always options.
   - I choose to keep going. I can do this.
   - I have the right to be happy and healthy.

- This feeling won't last forever. I need to get busy doing something constructive.
- I'm in charge of my feelings. I need to change my negative thoughts now.

6. Exercise.
7. Start a project that brings purpose or meaning to your life. Often, helping others in need is a good way to accomplish this.
8. Talk to a good, empathetic listener.
9. Write down your feelings of sadness.
10. Generate a list of things that make you happy and bring them into your day.
11. Consider medication and/or speaking with a therapist.

The next steps call for a little more investment in noticing your feelings. Overall, you'll likely find that attending to your emotional self does not take much time, just a firm and consistent commitment (more about this later). Try following this process to further develop your emotional awareness and insight:

1. Collect data on your feelings for one week. Four or five times each day, stop what you are doing and note any feelings, along with their intensity. Identify your thoughts about the situation at the time, and the thoughts that may have produced that feeling. At the end of the week, look for patterns in what you've recorded.
2. Now, collect data for four weeks. Yes, a whole month—just do it!! Spending a month making progress in educating yourself on your feelings is worth all the effort if it frees you from perpetually letting your feelings run your life. Remember, (a) it is your job to identify/know/own your feelings, and (b) your feelings are not going away. Those of you who think you "have no feelings" actually do, you

know; suppressing them is not only unhealthy but limits the quality of your life and stifles the depth of your relationships. Use this exercise to learn how to recognize your emotions.

3. Repeat the steps above until you are comfortably able to identify, know, and own your feelings and can verbalize them to others.

4. Then ask yourself the following questions:
   • How would you intellectually describe your emotional self?
   • How would you describe your general temperament?
   • Are your feelings constructive or counterproductive, both for you personally and for your relationship?
   • Are there ongoing stressors or temporary changes that could explain any unpleasant feelings? Remember, with any change comes emotional reaction, and the bigger the change, the bigger the emotional reaction is likely to be.
   • Are there any emotional issues you might need to resolve?

Hopefully, both you and your partner are invested in gaining knowledge and ownership of your emotions. When this is the case, you can try sharing your personal findings with each other, taking care to avoid comparing, critiquing, or arguing about each other's work. The purpose is to help you better accept each other's feelings and improve management of your own feelings in relation to your partner. If you can see patterns in how you react to your partner, and vice versa—e.g., you feel anxious, depressed, or angry when your partner acts a particular way—then you can better understand how to manage these feelings and resolve the related issues. Without some valid data from your partner, you may make decisions based on assumptions rather than valid information.

Once you have developed some conclusions from sharing this information, ask the following questions:

- What can you learn about your emotional reactions to your partner and his/her feelings?
- How would you describe your partner's general temperament?
- What level of stress or change is your partner experiencing that may account for some of his/her feelings?
- Do your emotional styles blend to produce a healthy emotional relationship?

If there are emotional issues to be resolved, each of you must do your part. Remember, you are partners in life and partners in business—partners who want to successfully own and manage this marriage.

Now pause for a minute to consider all the work you have done by collecting data about your own and your partner's feelings. It's quite an accomplishment, but it's not the end of your task; rather, it's just a part of the process. You are actually going to master this ability to recognize and manage your feelings and develop it into a life-long skill, one that you will practice—yes, that's right—your whole lifetime. The more consistently you identify, know, and own your feelings, the sooner you will develop a life-long routine that becomes easier and thus more automatic, and eventually integrates with your intellect.

Many people considering the work involved in gaining this insight have an issue with the time that appears to be involved. But although it has taken a number of pages to describe the process in writing, that does not mean practicing it will take up a significant amount of time in your schedule. In fact, you'll be able to complete all the necessary work in less time than it takes to watch your favorite TV show, fold the laundry, or wash the car. How much time **does** it take to track emotions during your day? The total time for periodic checks on your feelings typically comes to no more than five minutes a day. And the benefits will be huge! You'll find that gaining the use of your feelings will open up richer and more effective ways to approach life and make successful choices. Self-awareness and managing your feelings will improve the quality of your life while simplifying it. Remember, not only are you able to do this, you are responsible for doing it, because…you are the sole owner of your emotional world!

Mark and Alice

Mark and Alice are an older couple who have been married for five years now. This is the second marriage for both. Having had a few unsettlingly intense arguments, they have sought therapy to make sure their negative feelings do not overrule their commitment to make this marriage a permanent one. Both recognize they can be intensely hurt and angry. They communicate mostly by blaming or attacking each other. But both have also dedicated themselves to finding out how to recognize, label, and manage their own feelings.

They are learning to identify when to take a break and cool down; each is now aware that the actions or words of the other can spontaneously trigger emotions in themselves. They have also come to understand how quick they have been to make assumptions or mind-read the intentions of the other. Sometimes they seem to see their partner more as 'the enemy' than a loving spouse!

A process has begun to develop, one of calming down, then talking through what happened, each owning his or her part in the argument. The couple can now begin to learn how they might grow from, rather than stay wounded by, these emotional experiences. While they feel they are "taking two or three steps forward then one step backward," they continue to work on their common goal of intellectually taking charge of the damaging emotional reactions each of them brings to this relationship. As a result of their joint efforts to recognize, oversee, and manage their own emotions, they've grown closer and built a deeper, more loving partnership as two individuals who have found a way to prioritize their vision over their emotional power struggles. This has helped strengthen their commitment to stay married for life.

PART III
A Joint (Ad)Venture

Barring external events that come our way, we are responsible for the design, creation, and quality of our individual lives. When each of us is 85 (or 95!) years of age and looking back at the life we've led, the quality of that life will be largely a function of the choices, large and small, we have made. The responsibilities and rights of those choices begin with adulthood—in effect, at the age of 18. It becomes our duty (not our parents', caregivers', or any other person's) and our right to oversee and manage each and every facet of our lives. We must be aware of creating and maintaining an effective balance between what we want and what we need as we develop ourselves as individuals. We have the choice to take action and maximize the quality of the time we have here, or we can choose to coast and simply exist. Regardless, the choices we make have the potential to empower each of us to lead happy, fulfilled lives.

Balancing Self and Marriage

Marriage is one of the most significant choices available to us, and it is one that fundamentally impacts life in ways that are different from most other choices. This is primarily because marriage is bound by a legal contract that includes adhering to lifelong commitments and vows. Once made, the decision to marry affects the way we go about making many of our subsequent choices. Because we are acting for the good of our marriage, our decisions must be made through a merger of our individual vote and that of our partner, and therefore, a portion of our decisions are no longer independent ones. The balance of the decisions we make—those that involve developing our own lives while respecting the needs of our partner—must still allow us to be happy, enjoy life, and continue to view marriage as adding quality and value to our lives.

While there are a variety of reasons why people choose marriage, most people do so because they desire love, companionship, and the promise of a full, rich life shared with another person. All this adds up to the ideal picture of a stable, long-term partnership. And yet…50 percent of marriages fail. How is it that the quality of marriage becomes lost over time? Life, happiness, and hope are replaced by disappointment, bitterness, mistrust, and emptiness.

What is your definition of marriage? What was it you thought you were getting when you said your vows? When you chose marriage, did you have a vision, a plan for ensuring your marriage continued to be a quality choice for you? What, if anything, do you need to maintain a high quality of connection? Did you lose your sense of self at some point during your years together, or have you not ever had a well-defined identity where marriage could fill a part (not the whole) of your life? Over the years, have you simply not contributed enough to managing your marriage? In other words, have you taken your marriage for granted?

Imagine a company that is founded with much optimism and enthusiasm, but then fal-

Marriage is a Choice

- Marriage is not a substitute for one's self
- Marriage is not a requirement for one's life
- Marriage should add quality to one's life

ters because no one shows up to run the operation and keep the business going. The result is inevitable, painful, and unnecessary—truly a preventable failure. Life is short and most of us don't want to make choices that waste time on conflicts, friction, and arguing.

This book was written to help couples navigate the psychological complexities that arise when marriage comes into each person's life. The goal is to help couples thrive in their marriage, to enjoy the love of a partnership, and to fulfill the commitments made. We've looked at marriage from a business perspective and we've looked at its emotional side. Now it's time to talk about how to bring these two together. As your two lives merge and embrace one relationship, you both need to be involved in the design and development of that relationship. Success in your relationship will require applying your logical problem-solving and communication skills coupled with managing your emotional self.

Actively using the information described in Parts I and II will equip you with the necessary tools for this challenge. Here's how to set the stage for a balanced, psychologically healthy marriage: From Part I—an objective model using the basic fundamentals of business development—use tools to help you intellectually attend to yourself and the needs of the relationship. This will enable you to have more effective discussions, efficiently resolve conflicts, and make quick progress so you can move on to enjoying your relationship. From Part II—a condensed review of the components that make up emotional health—use tools for managing your emotions within your own self and within the context of your relationship. You will be well equipped to succeed in your efforts at self-management, and when both of you are practicing these techniques, the mechanics of overseeing the relationship will become more smooth and effortless.

No longer will one of you neglect to contribute intellectually, leaving your partner to take up the slack and eventually become overtaxed and resentful. Neither will one of you feel free to dominate the relationship, pushing the other into a position where he or she can only passively exist. Instead, by putting skills learned from the business model to work, both of you will find yourselves participating fully and equally, contributing ideas, plans, decisions, and productivity to your marriage. Likewise, practicing emotional management skills will result in a partnership where feelings of sadness, anger, or fear are not allowed to run unchecked, exhausting both of you and inhibiting the progress of your relationship. Instead, feelings will be dealt with in a constructive manner, opening the door for deeper insight and closer connection, and paving the way forward to a rewarding life together. There will be time, energy, and space for laughter and joy as you begin to truly enjoy your partnership and the fruits of your labor together.

Are you ready to start applying the information in this book directly to your relationship? How will this happen for you and your partner? What will be your first step and when will you begin? Maybe there is an issue that has been causing conflict in your marriage for some time and you have not been able to find a workable solution. Or maybe you need to make a joint decision in order to move forward, and you haven't been able to come to an agreement so far.

For a closer look at how you might seize these opportunities for growth, let's take a detailed look at the processes one married couple follow as they get down to the business of marriage.

Dylan and Kate

For seven months, Dylan and Kate have contemplated, argued, procrastinated, and silently steamed over their housing dilemma. They need to move—fast! Living in the basement efficiency apartment of Kate's parents' home was always meant to be a temporary measure, but their lack of agreement on money and just where to settle has kept them in limbo for what seems like forever. Now cramped quarters and frayed tempers are starting to affect not only the long-term quality of their marriage, but their relationship with Kate's parents as well.

It's time for some action, some change that will produce results. Dylan and Kate have decided to hold a board meeting with the goal of creating a workable process that makes it easier to successfully negotiate and compromise on the myriad of important decisions they know await them. Here's how they worked the program:

1. First, the couple scheduled a convenient time and place for their board meeting. They chose a Wednesday evening after work, knowing Kate's parents would be out until 10 pm so their privacy would be ensured. Prior to the meeting, both added items to the agenda list which was written on the legal pad they kept on the kitchen counter. The topic of the meeting was written at the top…"Finding a Way to Negotiate without Conflict."

2. At the start of the meeting, they sat down at their tiny kitchen table, eyeing each other a bit warily. Even though they had been married for four years, it was still hard trying something new and neither wanted to be the first to start! After a brief silence they began by agreeing to discuss the first item on the agenda, 'Dealing with deadlocks.' It was a tough one, and Dylan wrote out this short phrase and placed it on the table between them as a reminder to stay on task.

3. As the first speaker, Kate talked for less than a minute about her experience over the past seven months and then spent nearly three minutes outlining what she wanted to have happen in the future. She wanted them to intellectually, not emotionally, solve their dilemmas in a timely fashion so they could move forward and generate a plan for getting into their first home. She proposed a short series of steps involving negotiation and compromise, and tied

these to specific decisions involved in the purchase of their new home—how much to spend, how much to borrow, how far from work they will live. During her brief presentation of her point of view, she:

a. Opened with a clear statement of her objective and her supporting points.

b. Resolved to be assertive (not passive, not aggressive).

c. Stuck to the points on her list, which she had thought through before coming to the table.

d. Had a good grasp of what she wanted the outcome to be.

e. Used language that was constructive and positive.

4. While he listened to his wife, Dylan noticed a number of different emotions coming to the surface, one after the other. He jotted down a few words to remember these, but quickly returned his focus to what Kate was telling him. He was aware that the topic of this meeting was 'finding a way to negotiate without conflict'—it was not about his feelings or about getting into a power struggle. He was surprised to hear Kate say she actually agreed with his approach for gauging how much of a mortgage they should take on, as he had thought this was the area where they disagreed most. As she went on to express some of the fears she had around borrowing, he began to understand more fully why their past disagreements had been so entrenched. As he listened, Dylan:

a. Focused on gaining a clear understanding of Kate's points.

b. Reflected back to her occasionally, to make sure he'd got it right.

c. Sought to see the issue from Kate's perspective—especially, to see how and why she thought her position on borrowing was good for their marriage.

d. Did not interrupt, but waited for his turn to talk.

5. During the ensuing conversation, both Dylan and Kate covered a lot of ground. Their talk ranged from very direct, detailed, concrete facts and figures related to mortgage options, to abstract and intuitive expressions of long-held fears, anxieties, hopes, and expectations. They were able to successfully navigate both these conversational worlds by using **all** their business skills and self-management tools, such that they:

   a. Kept the focus on their goal which, again, was redirecting the conversation as needed so that progress was made on developing a workable process that allowed them to negotiate and compromise successfully and reach joint decisions when they disagreed.

   b. Stayed aware of their feelings, checking for any occurrence of 'sad, mad, or scared.'

   c. Freely used brainstorming techniques in order to open up their list of options during problem-solving.

   d. Made every effort to be respectful and nonjudgmental toward each other as they talked about the issue at hand.

   e. Stayed in touch with each other's emotional undertone and experience.

6. The couple continued to use effective communication skills, even when the going got rough. At one point, Dylan had to remind himself to use 'I sentences', and twenty minutes into the agenda, Kate realized she had wandered too far off topic and redirected the discussion to the issue on the piece of paper between them.

7. Throughout their interaction, both Dylan and Kate kept the general goals of their meeting and their partnership in mind as a positive context for their discussion and problem-solving. They reminded each other a couple of times that their efforts were all meant to help them enjoy their life together and strengthen their marriage.

8. By the end of their meeting, they had sorted out a three-step process for negotiating successfully which minimized their conflict and was comfortable enough for both of them to use when they realized they were going head-to-head over an issue and neither intended to give in. Both of them were happy with their accomplishments and were actually looking forward to their next board meeting and moving forward toward finding a home.

9. It took 70 minutes to get this far and they both agreed to call it a night. Business was finished; progress had been made. Life in their marriage is good.

What do you think of Dylan and Kate's approach? Can you see yourself and your spouse holding your version of a business meeting using your own personalized agenda? Perhaps it's time to give it a go. Keep a copy of your Partnership Tools handy for when you get stuck, and afterward, record some thoughts about how you managed yourself in the lines below.

Our first meeting:

_____

_____

_____

In addition, you can write down your thoughts about what you'd like to improve next time around.

Maintaining a professional, business-like approach:

_____

_____

_____

Self-managing emotions:

_____

_____

_____

You can also decide to share these notes with each other. This will help you both continue to grow in your own mastery of these skills, while building an awareness of each other's strengths and challenges. With practice, conducting business does get easier, especially if you are consistently using the tips, the skills, and the self-management tools. Remember to keep your eyes on the goal of building a mature partnership and a routine that works—one that will allow you to get the job done so you can go out, have fun, and enjoy life!

More Couple Stories

Here are more stories of how some couples have gotten into trouble in their marriage, and how they can change course. First, let's hear about how some are using the business tools described in Part I of this book:

1. Recently married, both Rex and Joanna have each been successful in their independent and professional lives. Faced with being co-leaders of their marriage, they've noted an increase in friction, conflict, and power struggles. Reviewing their definitions of marital partnership (ownership), clarifying their job descriptions (division of chores), and reaching a unified agreement will help strengthen the foundation they're building for their relationship.

2. Stacey hears her biological clock ticking and is ready to start a family. Rick's priorities are finishing school and building a comfortable nest egg before having children. While both of them share similar goals within their shared vision, their business plans are not aligned. Calling a board meeting to update and coordinate how they'll reach all of these goals as a team in a timely manner will get them back on track.

3. Both Taylor and Adam see themselves as rational, responsible business owners of their 25-year marriage. Occasionally, however, unexpected stressors cause challenges to the stability of their relationship. Wanting to minimize any stress, Taylor prefers to work out solutions by staging impromptu, spur-of-the-moment talks while Adam opts to resolve their dilemmas by making quick, snap decisions on his own. He informs Taylor of 'their' solutions as he's leaving for work, while watching TV, or through texting, and sometimes he neglects to inform her at all. Both seem to have forgotten they are partners, and solutions could be easily voted on and resolved in short, logically run board meetings. If they can professionally attend and contribute to staff meetings at their respective jobs, then they can do the same to resolve problems that confront the stability of their marriage.

4. Paul doesn't want to rock the boat with Susan so he doesn't speak up. Susan, on the other hand, is critical. She uses "You" sentences, talks down to him, and throws in words such as always, never, and should. She also often interrupts Paul, and doesn't appear to be truly listening to his statements. To create a better working partnership and make progress toward their common goals, Susan must learn to respect Paul's equal ownership role, improve her communication skills, and become a more active listener. Paul needs to be more assertive, comfortably practice his

equal ownership responsibilities and rights, and become proficient in the art of objective, intellectual, negotiating.

Now let's take a look at marriages that could benefit from more effective emotional self-management on the part of one or both partners, as explained in Part II:

1. Lynn enjoys a stable marriage and a rewarding career. Yet, she suffers from depression and low self-esteem and says she's reluctant to express her opinions in most situations for fear of ridicule and rejection. She has learned that her discomfort comes primarily not from external situations, but from her negative interpretations of how she approaches these situations. Through study and practice, she is now more comfortable being herself through staying aware of the negative, self-defeating thoughts she generates and choosing to develop a repertoire of positive statements that more accurately define her views and her role in life situations.

2. After dating for six months, Robyn and Zach began looking for an apartment and planning for marriage. Within weeks, Zach got cold feet, withdrew, and chose to spend more time with his male friends than with Robyn. He still professed his love for her and his desire to get married, but contributed little else to resolve the consequences of his shifting attitudes in their developing partnership. As Zach was probably becoming aware, marriage is a big, life-altering choice that is supposed to bring quality to both partners' lives. If he truly wants to add marriage to the balance of his life, he must identify and work through his fears and share his concerns with Robyn in an effective manner rather than become silent and absent from their emotional relationship. Doing so will help him with this dilemma as well as other upcoming life situations. Rather

than controlling or denying his emotional self, his task is
to choose to take charge and be responsible for his own
feelings and for his relationship to Robyn.

3. Eric's wife suggested he seek help when his highly successful career came to an abrupt end. Still needing to finan-
cially support his family, he didn't have the time or the
desire to understand the emotional toll his job loss took
on his health. As he spent long hours looking for work, he
dropped the exercise routine he enjoyed and began to eat.
He gained 50 pounds, developed high blood pressure and
high cholesterol, and had difficulty sleeping. It seems Eric
was never clearly in touch with his feelings, and will need
to develop some acceptance of how stress affects all of us
emotionally and physically. Additionally, he should be
willing to watch for subtle signs of anger, sadness, or anxiety as this will be key to restoring his health and keeping
his stress in check as he works to reinvent his career life.

4. Brenda and Max are happily married. Brenda is well-liked
by friends, family and the teachers at her children's school.
She appears to be a 'super mom' who is always smiling and
never says no, but who is also now constantly exhausted.
She's recently experienced attacks of anxiety which are a
cause of concern for her. Having stretched herself so thin,
she can't find a way to keep up with all she has committed to do and get rid of her mounting anxiety. The amount
of energy and time that Brenda now must devote to her
external obligations and reducing her anxiety and stress
drastically reduce the level of resources she can make
available to her marriage and family. It will take her some
time to reallocate her time and energy to first restore her
health, and then become able to once again contribute to
her home relationships. Brenda would benefit from being
able to take ownership of her feelings, learn ways to reduce
their intensity, and keep her anxiety at a low level. She also

has to choose to prioritize her emotional health above the demands of never-ending external challenges.

5. Shelley is afraid of anger and conflict and, therefore, controls some of her feelings of hurt and fear instead of managing them. Her husband, on the other hand, is not afraid to vent his feelings and expresses most of them, including anger, directly at her. The intimacy in their marriage is virtually nonexistent. Shelley's challenge is to learn the difference between controlling and managing her feelings, practice being more assertive, and learn not to take responsibility for her husband's feelings. If Shelley's husband wants the intimacy in their marriage to improve, he needs to stop holding his wife accountable for his unhappiness and maturely choose to practice and develop effective emotional self-management skills. Both need to consistently and continually do their part to rebuild and maintain the emotional partnership they used to enjoy.

6. Audrey is well liked by her family, friends, and colleagues. Her marriage of 17 years recently ended in divorce. On the surface, Audrey always appeared happy and willing to be available to all others at all times. She had neglected to notice that her husband, Nathan, had grown unhappy, resentful, and nonresponsive. Both independently sought to discover what had happened in the breakdown of their partnership and what they could learn about themselves as a result of this loss. Audrey still struggles with always acting happy when she really isn't; Nathan has difficulty understanding why she's making some progress and he's still depressed. Both could benefit from knowing that their thoughts govern their feelings and that their thoughts, not their feelings, will guide them to the answers they seek. Audrey wants to remain happy but without such a heavy load of obligations to others; Nathan wants to be happier and needs to learn what that means to him.

PART IV
Moving Forward

The world of psychology is much too complex to understand from any one self-help manual. This book is designed to simplify some of that complexity by (a) following practical precepts borrowed from the world of business, and (b) focusing on a key tenet of psychological self-management, namely the understanding and application of knowledge about the relationship between thoughts and feelings. Together, these steps make up a straightforward approach to making the most of your marriage.

The book also goes a step further to address issues relevant to the pursuit of love, happiness, and a satisfying quality of life. Within this context, the book portrays marriage as existing alongside and underlying each person's individual existence. While it requires a fair amount of time and attention, marriage can add richness and depth to life. At the same time, it will never serve as a substitute for one's individual self.

Your Commitment to Each Other

Do you remember the commitment statement that started this whole process? It forms the foundation for the first part of this book, and from it arise your first steps toward bringing structure and productive organization into your marriage. It also provides a vision that illuminates where you are heading as a couple and communicates a strong commitment to arrive there **together**:

We agree to become partners in joint ownership of a business with a vision and a plan, adopting policies and procedures which are developed during regularly scheduled board meetings and are achieved through skills of negotiating, compromising, and communicating.

When you read this statement, can you sense a mutual solidarity and dedication? Are there parts of your original wedding vows that compliment and further embellish your commitment to each other?

You are a team, with equal ownership in and equal responsibility for your marriage, and at this point you now have the tools you need to live up to your stated commitment. Because you have learned how business skills can be applied to help build your marital 'business', you are now well equipped for handling the practical side of marriage, and can feel confident that you have the necessary resources to accomplish your goals. If, however, a step toward making progress doesn't feel right or just seems too big to tackle, you may notice some resistance to continuing on with your efforts. Perhaps fear, frustration, or even downright apathy is signaling that your approach to change, to your marriage, or to owning your half of the partnership is not working. This is where the self-management skills you learned in the second part of this book can keep you from getting bogged down. What are your feelings telling you about the issues that are keeping you from making progress? And how will you use your thought processes to address these feelings and overcome the obstacles in your path to progress?

You have also learned how to use your feelings to guide you in knowing when a particular issue in your marriage needs to be addressed. When an emotional red flag is raised, remember: don't make assumptions; don't avoid or discount your feelings, your problems, or your spouse; don't take this significant part of your life for granted; and don't lean too heavily on a hopefulness that is simply not supported by the day-to-day reality of your lives. Instead, stay the course! Call a meeting, keep on top of issues, and make sure the goal of stabilizing your marriage remains a priority. Avoid putting things off until there is a setback or crisis; it may just be too little, too late. And remember, this is not hard work, it's just different work.

Marriage: The Big Picture

The institution of marriage has been around for ages. Throughout time, the reasons why people marry have always varied and while some are based on love (a shared affection, the desire to raise a family and grow old together, etc.), others are not (looking to carry on the family name, marrying for financial gain, etc.). In either case, the enormity of the decision to marry is frequently not well understood or realized until after the marriage vows are taken. The overwhelming experience of being deeply in love and the demands of planning a wedding celebration can mask the amount of work that lies ahead for a typical married couple. Most newlyweds enjoy a blissful honeymoon period steeped with love and romance. However, when that honeymoon period is over, marriage maintenance begins.

Regardless of what century, generation, or culture newlyweds come from, some marriages work for a lifetime and others don't. People dream, hope, and believe in the institution of marriage; they place a high value on marriage as a sign of success, fulfillment, or completion. Some men and women actively seek out marriage; they view it as a necessity, feel inadequate without it, and judge others regarding it. Overall, they spend a lot of time and energy on their marriage.

But what exactly is marriage and how can a person search for it when they can't see it? Marriage doesn't tangibly exist as a visible entity the way a house, restaurant, or school does. Instead, it is manifested through a relationship between two people. In fact, the written legal contract that establishes this relationship is the most tangible part of marriage. The two people involved have the right to create any vision of their relationship they might choose; hopefully, their vision is one that allows them to enjoy each other and their relationship for the rest of their lives.

One of the reasons this book was written was to help you visualize and build a marriage that brings a tangible reality to the life, love, and happiness you share with your spouse. Whether or not it is easy for you to embrace a business analogy for marriage, it offers one unique way to approach marriage from a mature and logical perspective, drawing on these qualities to enhance and compliment your loving feelings for each other.

Thinking of Getting Married?

For those readers who are considering getting married in the near future, remember that your time on this planet Earth is relatively short and thus it is vital that you **think** before you make this critical decision. As you consider 'taking the plunge', you will want to know exactly what it is that you're plunging into and everything about the one who is plunging with you. Start with identifying your own vision of marriage **and** your partner's. In our society, there are many varying views of what married life will look like, with significant—and often conflicting—differences drawn along cultural, religious, ethnic, and gender lines. These differences must be respected and carefully taken into consideration since such deeply established assumptions and beliefs are found in each of us and are resistant to change. They will influence your relationship whether or not you acknowledge and plan ahead for them.

The best time to create your marital vision is **before** the marriage ceremony. While the romance can continue, the honeymoon phase of your relationship eventually will dwindle and be replaced by the need to attend to the necessities of mundane, everyday duties such as going to work, managing finances, completing household chores, and more. In addition, there will be some new tasks that come specifically from being in a partnership. These involve the work of collaborating, coordinating, and engaging in joint planning processes where previously you made unilateral choices and decisions.

By all means enjoy your engagement, the parties, the preparation, and of course, the wedding. But don't let the celebrating keep you from addressing the realities that are crucial to building your dream life together. Ask yourselves the tough questions: Are you and your partner fully prepared to have marriage become a permanent factor in each of your lives, one that will forever change the quality of your time here? Do you believe your commitment to each other can survive all that life brings? Or will your marriage be susceptible to failure due to neglect, a lack of understanding, or an over-reliance on the sentimental notion that love is all you need? Having a vision and a plan will need to be followed by having the dedication to contribute to your marital 'company.' It is hoped you will use this book to plan the specific ways you and your future spouse will take action to ensure the survival of your relationship.

Seeking More for Your Established Marriage?

If you have already 'taken the plunge,' you most likely know a good deal about the reality of sustaining a marriage. You may have been married a year or two, or perhaps it's been twenty years or more. The longer you've been together, the more clearly you will be able to identify what it is that you both want—and how that differs from what you both thought you were getting when you said "I do!" If you're looking to build quality into your relationship, then lean on the old adage that "Where there's a will, there's a way." Two committed partners can turn a 'company' in need of a reorganization into a company that is a thriving success. But it does take two: two equal owners committed to compatible and similar goals for their joint company.

You have learned all about the technical side to this marital work, about how to use the logical business model as a guide for finding your own solutions and how to use negotiating and compromising skills to coordinate your own wishes with the desires of your spouse. You've learned how to communicate not only your love for one another, but also thoughts about the mundane aspects of daily life together as well as the vast array of life's topics, no matter how challenging they may be. You've even learned how to fight fair, as loving and equal partners who choose a quality marriage for life. You now have the information and skills needed to proceed with strengthening and safeguarding your marriage. The basic blueprint presented in the first part of this book will enable you to create a structure from which your relationship can stabilize and grow. Actively using the blueprint to build this structure will create stability, and allow you to develop over time the constancy and solidarity that all marriages crave.

If, in the process, you find some of the information in this book too complicated to tackle, don't give up or give in. Recognize the strength of your motivation to improve your marriage which has led you to read this book. Start with one of the small steps. For example, you could choose to study and practice information from just one specific section, and once you've mastered that, move on to another part. The work in this book is not necessarily hard, but for some it can certainly seem different. This may stem from being asked to apply what is already familiar to you (common business practices) in a new and unfamiliar way. However, if you tolerate the resultant discomfort and persevere in the process, you will be able to develop and maintain something of great value to you: your marriage. Married couples, if any of you have ever wanted to become an entrepreneur, now is your chance!

The Goal: Enjoying Life Together!

In closing, life is short and it is important. While we are here, we can choose to simply exist or to actively contribute to this world. Hopefully, this book helps some—maybe many—couples maximize the time they can spend enjoying each other!

Partnership Tools

Ownership Commitment Statement

We agree to become partners in joint ownership of a business with a vision and a plan, adopting policies and procedures which are developed during regularly scheduled board meetings and are achieved through skills of negotiating, compromising, and communicating.

Ownership Tips

GOAL: To break down the ownership commitment statement into memorable and manageable key components

REMEMBER:
- Two equal partners
- Sharing one agreed-upon vision and plan
- With scheduled board meetings
- And agreed-upon policies and procedures
- Developed through negotiating and compromising
- Using effective communication skills.

Board Meeting Tips

GOAL: To efficiently and consistently identify, discuss, and solve problems

STEPS:
- Agree upon a time and place.
- Create one agenda combining concerns identified by either or both partners.
- Work to promote the success of the marriage vision and plan.
- Identify what each partner will produce or contribute.

Power Plays and Giveaways

GOAL: To maintain a healthy and fair-minded approach that helps assure an equitable balance of power

POWER PLAYS:
- Talking down to the other person
- Interrupting
- Using intimidation tactics

POWER GIVEAWAYS
- Failing to offer input or suggestions
- Not preparing well enough
- Giving up, giving in

Straight Talk Tips

GOAL: To maximize the efficiency of discussions during business meetings

REMEMBER:
- Stay focused
- Stick to the subject
- Keep on track
- No emotional venting
- Don't give up

Negotiating Tips

GOAL: To negotiate with business-like skill and effectiveness

STEPS:

- Use logic, not emotions, to resolve differences.
- Know your position on each point being discussed. Be able to explain how your position benefits the vision and plan for your marriage.
- Expect your partner's opinion to be different than yours (otherwise, why would there be a need to negotiate?).
- Listen, understand, and know the value of your partner's position as it relates to the marital vision and plan.
- Focus on achieving a fair solution, not defending your position.
- Be flexible, know options, offer alternatives.
- Be prepared to say no and to hear no from your partner. Alternative options need to be offered.
- Use assertiveness; don't be passive or aggressive.
- In the event of an impasse, consider rescheduling and trying later.

Communication Tips

GOAL: To bring clarity and respect into discussions

STEPS:
- DO stay focused, stick to the topic.
- DO listen carefully and respectfully.
- DO respond empathically; try to see the other's point of view.
- DO use "I" sentences instead of "You" sentences.
- DO take a time out if there is a breakdown in communications.
- DO stick with the facts instead of mere opinion.

- DON'T give up.
- DON'T try to win or be right—that's a power play.
- DON'T interrupt, it's part of always being respectful toward your partner.
- DON'T resort to giving anyone the 'silent treatment'.
- DON'T mind read, blame, keep score, get defensive, sit passively or become aggressive.
- DON'T label, call names, or use any of the following words: should, ought, always, or never.

Categories of Daily Living

GOAL: To keep in balance all factors that contribute to a full and rewarding lifestyle

CATEGORIES:
- Physical, emotional, and spiritual well-being
- Relationship stability
- Financial stability
- Home management
- Career and professional goals
- Family health
- Personal interests
- Parenting practices
- Recreational and leisure activities

Partnership Responsibilities

GOAL: To identify the individual and shared responsibilities within a marriage partnership

RESPONSIBILITIES:

- Both partners intellectually manage the vision and the plan for the relationship.
- Each partner intellectually manages his/her own vision and plan (to be blended with the partnership vision).
- Each partner intellectually manages his/her own feelings.

Assertiveness Tips

GOAL: To use assertive techniques to advocate for yourself without slipping into aggression or passivity

STEPS:
- Maintain good body posture and eye contact.
- State clearly and directly what you want or believe.
- Start your sentences with "I".
- Manage your emotional reactivity.

REMEMBER:
- I have the right to be treated fairly and with respect.
- I have the right to be happy.
- I have the right to my feelings, beliefs, and my choices.
- I have the right to manage myself and not be responsible for my partner's thoughts, feelings, or behaviors.
- I have the right to say 'no' and not feel guilty.
- I have the right to express my opinions and ideas.
- I have the right to change my mind.
- I have the right to make mistakes.
- I have the right to say I don't know.
- I have the right to walk away if this is in my best interest.

Thoughts vs. Feelings Tips

GOAL: To correctly distinguish thoughts from feelings

STEPS:
- Separate thoughts and feelings into two distinct points within one sentence:

    For example: I feel _____ because I think _____.

    Incorrect= I feel like you're never going to change.
    Correct=I feel sad because I don't think you will change.

    Incorrect=I feel like you don't trust me.
    Correct=I feel sad because I don't think you trust me.

    Incorrect=I feel like we never get along.
    Correct=I feel sad because I don't think we get along.

- Own your thoughts and feelings.

    For example: I feel angry when you _____ .

    I feel hurt when you _____ .

    I feel frightened when you _____ .

    Incorrect=You make me mad.
    Correct=I'm mad because of something you did (or said).

    Incorrect=You hurt my feelings.
    Correct=I feel hurt by something you did (or said).

Incorrect=You're scaring me.

Correct=I feel scared because of what you are doing (or saying).

Feelings Management Tips

GOAL: To access and draw on information provided by emotional experiences while keeping the emotions themselves in perspective

STEPS:
- Consistently monitor the presence and intensity of your feelings (e.g., sad, mad, scared).
- Use management options to keep intensity low. On a 10-point scale where 10 is very intense and 1 is very low intensity, try to keep your intensity at a 3 or less.
- Take a break if your feelings begin to overrule your problem-solving skills.
- If needed, vent, process, or release your feelings at a later time (i.e., it's not healthy to avoid, deny, or suppress feelings indefinitely).

Marriage Is A Choice

GOAL: To develop a healthy and balanced perspective on marriage

REMEMBER:
- Marriage is not a substitute for one's self.
- Marriage is not a requirement for living.
- Marriage should add quality to one's life.

About the Authors

Jenny Secrest, PhD

Jenny Secrest is a psychologist who has worked to help individuals, couples, and families solve psychological dilemmas for more than 20 years. Her passion is to educate individuals, from childhood through adulthood, on practical and useful psychological information, such as self-management of thoughts and feelings. Dr. Secrest encourages school systems to introduce these kinds of skills during early childhood and expand on them through the high-school years. She is also dedicated to raising awareness of the consequences of childhood bullying and the importance of teaching children their psychological and legal rights.

Karin H. Bruckner, MA

Karin Bruckner is a freelance writer and researcher with a Master's degree in Psychology. Her clients are a diverse mix of organizations and individuals from both the US and New Zealand. She is the co-author of two books, and has carried out data collection and analyses for a variety of research projects. She is married and enjoys staying closely connected with her large blended family.

Made in the USA
Charleston, SC
26 May 2013